Through the Mysteries of Light with Giotto and Fra Angelico

Dedicated to

His Eminence, Francis Cardinal George, OMI

Visit our web site at
WWW.ALBAHOUSE.ORG

or call 1-800-343-2522 (ALBA)
and request current catalog

Through the Mysteries of Light with
Giotto and Fra Angelico

COMPILED BY GARY T. JOHNSON
EDITED BY EDMUND C. LANE, SSP

ST PAULS

Scripture passages from The New Testament: St. Paul Catholic Edition (ST PAULS / Alba House, 2000)

Illustrations:

Page 16 Giotto di Bondone (1266-1336). Baptism of Christ.
Copyright Alinari / Art Resource, NY
Scrovegni Chapel, Padua, Italy

Page 18 Giotto di Bondone (1266-1336). The Wedding at Cana.
Copyright Cameraphoto Arte, Venice / Art Resource, NY
Scrovegni Chapel, Padua, Italy

Page 20 Giotto di Bondone (1266-1336). The Resurrection of Lazarus.
Copyright Cameraphoto Arte, Venice / Art Resource, NY
Scrovegni Chapel, Padua, Italy

Page 22 Angelico, Fra (1387-1455). Transfiguration Fresco.
Copyright Scala / Art Resource, NY
Museo di San Marco, Florence, Italy

Cover and Page 24
Giotto di Bondone (1266-1336). The Last Supper.
Copyright Alinari / Art Resource, NY
Scrovegni Chapel, Padua, Italy

Produced and designed in the United States of America by the Fathers and Brothers of the Society of St. Paul, 2187 Victory Boulevard, Staten Island, New York 10314-6603, as part of their communications apostolate.

ISBN: 0-8189-0950-1

© *Copyright 2003 by the Society of St. Paul*

Printing Information:

Current Printing - first digit   1   2   3   4   5   6   7   8   9   10

Year of Current Printing - first year shown

2003   2004   2005   2006   2007   2008   2009   2010   2011   2012

Foreword[1]

How the Rosary Came Into Being

The Rosary as we know it hails from the High Middle Ages where it came into being in various medieval monasteries as a substitute for the recitation of the Divine Office on the part of those lay monks and devout lay persons who didn't know how to read. Instead of the 150 psalms, these would recite 150 "Our Father"s which they counted off on a ring of beads which came to be called by various names in different places: a "crown" of beads or "corona" being the most common appellation.

With the growth in popularity of Marian devotion, which reached its peak in the twelfth century, and with the widespread use of the "Hail Mary" — originally a liturgical antiphon for the Fourth Sunday of Advent made up of just the first part of the prayer — the "Psalter of the Blessed Virgin" composed of 150 "Hail Mary"s came into being alongside the "Psalter of the Father." Its diffusion was such that, for all practical purposes, in a very short time it completely supplanted the latter.

It's important to note that the origin of the Rosary was closely related to the Liturgy and, placed in the hands of the unlettered, made it possible for the average person to participate in the prayers recited by the monks in the choir. The universal popularity of this "Marian Psalter" encouraged many to enrich it, building on its original simple repetitive structure. This be-

---

[1] From *Through the Rosary with Fra Angelico* by Domenico Marcucci (Alba House, 1989).

gan with a young German by the name of Henry Kalkar (1328-1408) who subdivided the 150 "Hail Mary"s into 15 decades, separated by recitation of one "Our Father." A confrere of his, Dominic of Prussia, sometime prior to 1410, proposed a Rosary made up of 50 "Hail Mary"s in which to each "Hail Mary," after the name of Jesus — with which the original prayer ended — a phrase or clause which referred to an episode in the life of Jesus or of the Blessed Virgin would be added: 14 treating the hidden life, 6 referring to the public life, 24 dealing with the passion of Jesus and 6 covering the episodes following His resurrection. Thus the triple division of the mysteries of the Rosary into the *Joyful,* the *Sorrowful* and the *Glorious* was born.

This proposal of Dominic of Prussia met with almost immediate success and during the 1400's assisted in an extraordinary flowering of the Rosary. The mysteries eventually numbered as many as 300 and embraced the entire history of salvation, beginning with creation.

The Work of the Dominicans

The one who contributed more than any other to the launching of the Rosary and who conferred on it that structure with which it has come down to us today was the Dominican friar Alanus de Rupe (1428-1478). His work took place on several levels. First of all, he reformed the prayers, giving the greatest importance to the meditative element, which he called "the soul of the Rosary," rather than to the vocal part which constituted "the body." He divided the episodes in the history of salvation into three sets of fifty, the Joyful, the Sorrowful and the Glorious mysteries, each of which was further subdivided into five decades corresponding to our present-day fifteen decades — to which Pope John Paul II added five more on October 16, 2002.

Alanus de Rupe "ennobled" the whole by attributing the origin of the "Psalter of the Blessed Virgin" to St. Dominic — something that is historically unsubstantiated — and thus spurred his confreres on to make their own the apostolate of the Rosary. The Dominicans have, in fact, since then always propagated its recitation with notable results.

But Friar Alanus was above all an apostle, an outstanding preacher of popular missions, especially in the region of the Netherlands and northern Germany. During these missions he was tireless in his efforts at organizing Confraternities of the Rosary, presenting this prayer as a sure means to grow in the faith and as a powerful weapon against the enemies of the Church.

This last conviction was of extreme importance, so much so that it is spoken of in the first of the papal bulls on the Rosary to come down to us (*Ea quae,* of Sixtus IV, dated May 12, 1479). In it the Rosary is presented as "a pious and devout way of praying, which consists of reciting the angel's salutation every day — in honor of God and of the Blessed Virgin Mary, and against the dangers which threaten the world — as many times as there are Psalms in the Psalter of David." Moreover we cannot overlook how often these Confraternities of the Rosary validly resisted the inroads of Protestantism, so much so that this prayer has almost become a symbol of the Catholic faith.

Finally, this conviction was in a certain way historically confirmed in the victory of Lepanto (October 7, 1571), which Pope St. Pius V attributed more to the "arms" of the Rosary than to the power of the cannons and the valor of the soldiers who fought there. He even went so far as to establish October 7th, the day of the victory, as the day on which the Feast of the Most

Holy Rosary would be celebrated throughout the universal Church.

The definitive structure of the Rosary, which then became codified in the bull *Consueverunt Romani Pontifices,* was given by Albert di Castello, likewise a Dominican friar. He refined this pious practice even further, by suggesting material to be added between each "Hail Mary" as a simple aid to meditation.

During the period of the Renaissance, there were several forms of the Rosary in use far and wide by various religious congregations. Among these the "Rosary of the Seven Sorrows of Mary" recommended by the Servites enjoyed a certain favor. The form which ultimately prevailed, however, was that promoted by the Dominican Order and hailed by a large number of papal documents beginning with the cited *Consueverunt Romani Pontifices* of Pope St. Pius V. The Rosary is presented by it as "the veneration of the Blessed Virgin through the repetition of the angelic salutation 150 times, according to the number of the Psalms of David, interrupting each decade with an 'Our Father' and some specific meditations which illustrate the whole life of Our Lord Jesus Christ." Regarding the fruits of the Rosary, the bull was most eloquent indeed: "The faithful who fervently took this prayer to heart, inflamed by its meditations, were transformed into other persons; the darkness of heresy retreated and the light of the Catholic faith made strides once again."

The Rosary and the Life of a Christian

Down through the centuries this prayer, so apparently simple and disarming, has become the focal point of a whole series of values that are symbols, not only of Marian devotion but also of Catholicism itself. The Rosary is a prayer loved by the poor and the rich alike, the unlettered as well as the wise. It has inspired poets, apostles, saints and martyrs. Many have given their lives for Christ clutching the beads of the Rosary in their hands.

The unforgettable Pope John XXIII, uncompromising in his own fidelity to the daily recitation of the Rosary, described in a discourse on May 8, 1963 the milieu created by the common recitation of this prayer around the family hearth: "A poetic atmosphere which places before our eyes the sweet figure of the Madonna is created, the mysteries of the life of Our Lord are made familiar to all, and the challenges of Jesus with respect to our life are caused to be intensely felt…. When this prayer is recited in common one begins to absorb something of what will later become the proper direction for his or her own life." This little booklet has as its aim not only to represent the prayers of the Rosary, thus reaffirming their validity, but also to help one to draw close to the spirit of the Rosary, thus recovering something of the creative faith of such a prayer. Hence the text under each artistic representation announces the mystery that is the subject of that decade's meditation. This is anything but new. Indeed, it is a return to the sources, when the Rosary was first proposed as an aid to deepening and living one's faith.

This form of reciting the Rosary is mentioned and implicitly praised in Pope Paul VI's *Marialis Cultus*: "It is to be noted that, for the precise purpose of favoring contemplation and to help the mind correspond to the words being used, it was the practice at one time and the custom has been kept in several places — to add to the name of Jesus in every "Hail Mary" a phrase which would recall the mystery that had been announced" (n. 46).

The Rosary, then, is far more varied and complex than what it might at first seem and can, therefore, constitute a prayer adapted to the most diverse circumstances and persons: from a "prayer always at hand" according to a very perceptive expression of a Protestant pastor from Germany, Manfred Seitz to a highly efficacious aid to contemplation.

Finally, taking into account that many will be approaching the Rosary as a totally new prayer for them, both in the writing of the text and in the graphic presentation of the mysteries, we tried to be as clear as possible, indicating in some detail exactly how the prayer unfolds.

The Mysteries of Light

On October 16, 2002, Pope John Paul II wrote an Apostolic Letter entitled *Rosarium Virginis Mariae* in which he proclaimed October 2002 to October 2003 "The Year of the Rosary." In beginning the 25th year of his Pontificate, he wanted in this way to thank the Lord and his Most Holy Mother for the many graces he had received in the course of his life and ministry through the Rosary. At the same time he thought it opportune, in light of the special needs of the people of the Twenty-First Century, to suggest the addition of five new decades to the Rosary to encourage meditation on the public life of Jesus. He called these new mysteries, The Mysteries of Light. The following paragraphs are excerpted from his Letter.

The whole mystery of Christ is a mystery of light. He is the "light of the world" (Jn 8:12). Yet this truth emerges in a special way during the years of his public life, when he proclaims the Gospel of the Kingdom. In proposing to the Christian community five significant moments — "luminous" mysteries — during this phase of Christ's life, I think that the following can be fittingly singled out: (1) his Baptism in the Jordan, (2) his self-manifestation at the wedding of Cana, (3) his proclamation of the Kingdom of God, with his call to conversion, (4) his Transfiguration, and finally, (5) his institution of the Eucharist, as the sacramental expression of the Paschal Mystery.

Each of these mysteries is a *revelation of the Kingdom now present in the very person of Jesus.* The Baptism in the Jordan is first of all a mystery of light. Here, as Christ descends into the waters, the innocent one who became "sin" for our sake (cf. 2 Cor 5:21), the heavens open wide and the voice of the Father declares him the beloved Son (cf. Mt 3:17 and parallels), while the Spirit descends on him to invest him with the mission which he is to carry out. Another mystery of light is the first of the signs, given at Cana (cf. Jn 2:1-12), when Christ changes water into wine and opens the hearts of the disciples to faith, thanks to the intervention of Mary, the first among believers. Another mystery of light is the preaching by which Jesus proclaims the coming of the Kingdom of God, calls to conversion (cf. Mk 1:15) and forgives the sins of all who draw near to him in humble trust (cf. Mk 2:3-13; Lk 7:47-48): the inauguration of that ministry of mercy which he continues to exercise until the end of the world, particularly through the Sacrament of Reconciliation which he has entrusted to his Church (cf. Jn 20:22-23). The mystery of light *par excellence* is the Transfiguration, traditionally believed to have taken place on Mount Tabor. The glory of the Godhead shines forth from the face of Christ as the Father commands the astonished Apostles to "listen to him" (cf. Lk 9:35 and parallels) and to prepare to experience with him the agony of the Passion, so as to come with him to the joy of the Resurrection and a life transfigured by the Holy Spirit. A final mystery of light is the institution of the Eucharist, in which Christ offers his body and blood as food under the signs of bread and wine, and testifies "to the end" his love for humanity (Jn 13:1), for whose salvation he will offer himself in sacrifice.

In these mysteries, apart from the miracle at Cana, *the presence of Mary remains in the background.* The Gospels make only the briefest reference to her occasional presence at one moment or other during the preaching of Jesus (cf. Mk 3:31-5; Jn 2:12), and they give no indication that she was present at the Last Supper and the institution of the Eucharist. Yet the role she assumed at Cana in some way accompanies Christ throughout his ministry. The revelation made directly by the Father at the Baptism in the Jordan and echoed by John the Baptist is placed upon Mary's lips at Cana, and it becomes the great maternal counsel which Mary addresses to the Church of every age: "Do whatever he tells you" (Jn 2:5). This counsel is a fitting introduction to the words and signs of Christ's public ministry and it forms the Marian foundation of all the "mysteries of light".

How to Recite the Rosary

Many persons like to begin the recitation of the Rosary with the sign of the cross and the prayer:

V. O God, come to my assistance.
R. O Lord, make haste to help me.
Glory be to the Father, and to the Son and to the Holy Spirit, as it was in the beginning, is now, and ever shall be world without end. Amen.

After the *Glory be* it has become customary in many places to recite this prayer, which traces its origin to the apparitions at Fatima (May - October, 1917):

O my Jesus, forgive us our sins, save us from the fires of hell. Take all souls to heaven, especially those who have most need of your mercy.

Taking the crucifix of the Rosary in hand, the Creed is then recited:

I believe in God, the Father almighty,
Creator of heaven and earth;
And in Jesus Christ, His only Son, our Lord;
Who was conceived by the Holy Spirit,
Born of the Virgin Mary,
Suffered under Pontius Pilate,
Was crucified, died and was buried;
He descended into hell;
The third day, He rose again from the dead;
He ascended into heaven and sits at the right hand
  of God, the Father almighty;

*From whence He shall come to judge
  the living and the dead.
I believe in the Holy Spirit;
The holy Catholic Church;
The communion of saints;
The forgiveness of sins;
The resurrection of the body;
And life everlasting. Amen.*

The five beads that follow can be used to recite an *Our Father,* three *Hail Marys* to obtain the three theological gifts of faith, hope and charity, and a *Glory be*. The mystery of the first decade is then announced, using the traditional text as found beneath each illustration. This may be followed by a reading of the biblical citation and the enunciation of the intentions for which the decade is being offered. When only one Rosary is being recited during the day, then, the Holy Father suggests in his Apostolic Letter *Rosarium Virginis Mariae*, on Mondays and Saturdays it would be appropriate to recite the *Joyful Mysteries*; on Tuesdays and Fridays, the *Sorrowful*; on Wednesdays and Sundays, the *Glorious*; and on Thursdays, the *Mysteries of Light*. Each decade begins with an *Our Father,* followed by 10 *Hail Marys,* a *Glory be,* and the prayer, *O my Jesus*.

The five beads at the end of the Rosary leading back to the crucifix are sometimes used for the recitation of a *Hail Holy Queen,* and *Our Father, Hail Mary,* and *Glory be* for the intentions of the Holy Father, followed by an *Act of Contrition*.

For an even more reflective and meditative recitation, everything unfolds as above except that, following the name of Jesus in each *Hail Mary,* the corresponding phrase found in this little booklet is added. The second part of the prayer *Holy Mary,*

Mother of God, pray for us sinners, now and at the hour of our death is said only after the 10th *Hail Mary* and just before the *Glory be*. This is the style that was followed in the very popular companion to this booklet, *Through the Rosary with Fra Angelico* by Domenico Marcucci (Alba House, 1989).

It is likewise the style recommended by Pope John Paul II in his Apostolic Letter *Rosarium Virginis Mariae*: "The center of gravity in the *Hail Mary*, the hinge as it were which joins its two parts, is the *name of Jesus*. Sometimes, in hurried recitation, this center of gravity can be overlooked, and with it the connection to the mystery of Christ being contemplated. Yet it is precisely the emphasis given to the name of Jesus and to his mystery that is the sign of a meaningful and fruitful recitation of the Rosary. Pope Paul VI drew attention, in his Apostolic Exhortation *Marialis Cultus*, to the custom in certain regions of highlighting the name of Christ *by the addition of a clause referring to the mystery being contemplated*. This is a praiseworthy custom, especially during public recitation. It gives forceful expression to our faith in Christ directed to the different moments of the Redeemer's life. It is at once a profession of faith and an aid in concentrating our meditation, since it facilitates the process of assimilation to the mystery of Christ inherent in the repetition of the Hail Mary."

FIRST MYSTERY OF LIGHT

His Baptism in the Jordan

Jesus humbly consents to be baptized by John the Baptist in the waters of the Jordan River, investing him with the mission that he is to carry out and revealing the mystery of the Trinity.

Biblical Citation

At that time Jesus came from Galilee to be baptized by John at the Jordan. John tried to prevent him and said, "*I need to be baptized by you, and you are coming to me?*" But in answer Jesus said to him, "Let it be, for now — it is fitting for us to fulfill all God's will in this way." Then he let him. After he was baptized Jesus at once came up from the water and, behold, the heavens were opened and he saw the Spirit of God descending upon him like a dove. And, behold a voice from Heaven said, "This is My Beloved Son in whom I am well pleased." (Mt 3:13-17)

Prayer Intentions

- For peace.
- For missionaries everywhere.

Our Father...

Hail Mary, full of grace, the Lord is with you. Blessed are you among women, and blessed is the fruit of your womb, JESUS...

1 ... who came from Galilee to John at the Jordan, to be baptized by him.
2 ... whom John the Baptist called "The Lamb of God, who takes away the sin of the world."
3 ... who overcame John's reluctance by humbly fulfilling everything laid down by God.
4 ... who descended into the waters.
5 ... for whom the heavens opened up wide.
6 ... whom the Father declared to be his Beloved Son.
7 ... on whom the Spirit descended like a dove and remained on him.
8 ... whose baptism prepares us to receive the Messiah according to God's plan.
9 ... who made us truly members of the Lord's body.
10 ... who baptizes, not with water, but with the Holy Spirit.

Holy Mary, Mother of God, pray for us sinners, now and at the hour of our death. Amen.

Glory be... O my Jesus...

SECOND MYSTERY OF LIGHT

His Self-Manifestation at the Wedding Feast of Cana

the first of the signs took place at Cana when Christ changed water into wine and opened the hearts of the disciples to faith, thanks to the intervention of Mary, the first among believers.

Biblical Citation

On the third day there was a wedding in Cana of Galilee, and Jesus' mother was there. Now Jesus and his disciples had also been invited to the wedding, and when the wine ran out Jesus' mother said to him, "They have no wine." Jesus replied, "What do you want from me, woman? My hour hasn't come yet." His mother said to the servants, "Do whatever he tells you." Now six stone water jars were standing there, in accordance with the Jewish purification rites, each holding twenty to thirty gallons. Jesus said to them, "Fill the water jars with water." And they filled them to the brim. Then he said to them, "Now draw some out and take it to the head steward." So they took it. When the head steward tasted the water which had become wine… [he] called the bridegroom and said to him, "Every man first puts out the good wine, then when they're drunk he puts out the lesser wine; *you've* kept the good wine till *now*!" Jesus did this, the first of his signs, at Cana in Galilee and revealed his glory and his disciples believed in him. (Jn 2:1-11)

Prayer Intentions

- For the family.
- For those who serve God in their workplaces.

Our Father…

Hail Mary, full of grace, the Lord is with you. Blessed are you among women, and blessed is the fruit of your womb, JESUS…

1 … whose presence blesses love between man and woman, joined in marriage.
2 … of whom you were the first among believers.
3 … to whom you pointed out your concern.
4 … who heeded your intercession.
5 … of whom, you said: "Do whatever he tells you."
6 … whose words the servants obeyed precisely.
7 … who was the good wine, held back until the right time.
8 … whose gift was generous, filled to the brim.
9 … who opens our hearts to faith.
10 … whose signs reveal his glory.

Holy Mary, Mother of God, pray for us sinners, now and at the hour of our death. Amen.

Glory be… O my Jesus…

THIRD MYSTERY OF LIGHT

His Proclamation of the Kingdom of God, with His Calls to Conversion

by his preaching and miracles Jesus proclaims the Kingdom
of God, calls to conversion, and forgives the sins
of all who draw near to him in humble trust.

Biblical Citation

After John was arrested, Jesus came into Galilee proclaiming the good news of God, saying, "The appointed time has come and the Kingdom of God is at hand; repent and believe in the good news!" (Mk 1:14-15)

When he saw the crowds, he went up the mountain. After he sat down his disciples came to him, and he opened his mouth and taught them, saying, "Blessed are the poor in spirit, for theirs is the Kingdom of Heaven." (Mt 5:1-3)

Martha said to Jesus, "Lord, if you'd been here my brother would not have died, but even now I know that whatever you ask God for, God will give you." Jesus said to her, "Your brother will rise!" Martha said to him, "I know that he will rise at the resurrection on the last day." Jesus said to her, "I am the resurrection and the life! Whoever believes in me, even if he should die, will live, and everyone who lives and believes in me shall never die." (Jn 11:21-26)

"But so that you may know that the Son of Man has authority on earth to forgive sins" — he said to the paralytic — "Stand up, pick up your mat and go home." (Mk 2:10-11)

Prayer Intentions

- For the sick and for caregivers.
- For the conversion of sinners and the reevangelization of the faith in historically Christian areas.

Our Father…

Hail Mary, full of grace, the Lord is with you. Blessed are you among women, and blessed is the fruit of your womb, JESUS…

1 … who called the Apostles, making them fishers of men.
2 … who taught as one with authority, and not as the scribes.
3 … who healed the sick, restored sight to the blind and forgave sinners.
4 … who proclaimed the Kingdom of God.
5 … who showed a special love for the poor and needy.
6 … to whom the crowds came in faith, seeking healing.
7 … who blesses those who have not seen, and yet believe.
8 … who called blessed the peacemakers and those persecuted for his sake.
9 … who calls us to make disciples of all nations.
10 … who will be with us always, to the end of the age.

Holy Mary, Mother of God, pray for us sinners, now and at the hour of our death. Amen.

Glory be… O my Jesus…

FOURTH MYSTERY OF LIGHT

His Transfiguration

Jesus takes three of his disciples with him to the top of a high mountain and he is transfigured before them, preparing them to experience the agony of the Passion and giving them a foretaste of the joy of his glorious Resurrection.

Biblical Citation

About eight days after he spoke these words he took Peter, John, and James and went up the mountain to pray. And it happened that while he was praying the appearance of his face was altered, and his clothing became a dazzling white. And, behold, two men were speaking with him, Moses and Elijah, who were seen in glory speaking about his Exodus, which he would bring to completion in Jerusalem. Peter as well as those with him had been overcome by sleep, but when they were fully awake they saw his glory and the two men standing with him. And it happened that as Moses and Elijah were leaving him Peter said to Jesus, "Master, it's good for us to be here; let us put up three dwellings, one for you, one for Moses, and one for Elijah" — he didn't really know what he was saying. As he was saying this, a cloud arose and overshadowed them; then they were afraid as they entered the cloud. And a voice came from the cloud, saying, "This is My Son, My Chosen; hear him!" (Lk 9:28-35)

Prayer Intentions

- That we may be prepared for our own suffering and tribulation.
- That we may see God face-to-face in glory.

Our Father…

Hail Mary, full of grace, the Lord is with you. Blessed are you among women, and blessed is the fruit of your womb, JESUS…

1 … who led Peter, James and John up a high mountain apart.
2 … whose face shone like the sun and whose garments became white as light.
3 … with whom Moses and Elijah were talking.
4 … who was overshadowed by a cloud.
5 … of whom the Father said: "This is My Son, My Chosen; hear him!"
6 … before whom the disciples fell on their knees, filled with awe.
7 … who touched his disciples, saying, "Rise, and have no fear."
8 … who spoke of his own departure — his Passion, Death and Resurrection.
9 … who is endowed with glory and majesty in Heaven.
10 … who gives power to become children of God to all who believe in his name.

Holy Mary, Mother of God, pray for us sinners, now and at the hour of our death. Amen.

Glory be… O my Jesus…

FIFTH MYSTERY OF LIGHT

His Institution of the Eucharist, the Sacramental Reenactment of the Paschal Mystery

Christ institutes the Eucharist on the night when he was betrayed, offering his body and blood as food under the signs of bread and wine, commanding us to do this in remembrance of him.

Biblical Citation

When the hour came he sat down at table with the apostles. And he said to them, "With what longing have I longed to eat this Passover with you before I suffer, for I tell you that I will not eat it again until it is fulfilled in the Kingdom of God." Then he took a cup, blessed it, and said, "Take this and divide it among yourselves, for I tell you I will not drink the fruit of the vine from this moment until the Kingdom of God comes." Then he took bread, blessed it, broke it, and gave it to them, saying, "This is my body which is given up for you — do this in my remembrance." Likewise he took the cup after they had eaten and said, "This cup is the new covenant in my blood which is poured out for you." (Lk 22:14-20)

Prayer Intentions

- For a greater love and appreciation of the real presence of Christ in the Eucharist.
- For holy vocations to the priesthood and religious life.

Our Father…

Hail Mary, full of grace, the Lord is with you. Blessed are you among women, and blessed is the fruit of your womb, JESUS…

1 … who knew that his hour had come to depart from this world and go to the Father.
2 … who gave thanks to God on the night before he died.
3 … who instituted the Eucharist for the nourishment of our souls.
4 … who offered his body for us and inaugurated the new covenant in his blood.
5 … who told us to "Do this in remembrance of me."
6 … whose death we proclaim until he comes as often as we eat this bread and drink this wine.
7 … who offered himself in sacrifice for our salvation.
8 … who offers consolation and strength to us in the Eucharist.
9 … who, having loved his own who were in the world, loved them to the end.
10 … who remains with us always in the Blessed Sacrament of our altars.

Holy Mary, Mother of God, pray for us sinners, now and at the hour of our death. Amen.

Glory be… O my Jesus…

Salve Regina

Hail, holy Queen, Mother of mercy,
Our life, our sweetness and our hope,
To you do we cry, poor banished children of Eve;
To you do we sigh, mourning and weeping in this valley of tears.
Turn, then, most gracious advocate,
Your eyes of mercy toward us.
And after this, our exile,
Show unto us the blessed fruit of your womb, Jesus.
O clement, O loving, O sweet virgin Mary.

V.   Pray for us, O holy Mother of God.
R.   That we may be made worthy of the promises of Christ.

Let us pray. Pour forth, we beseech you, O Lord, your grace into our hearts, that we to whom the Incarnation of Christ, your Son, was made known by the message of an angel — may, by his passion and cross, be brought to the glory of his resurrection, through the same Christ, our Lord. Amen.

Litany of the Blessed Virgin Mary

Lord, have mercy on us. *Lord, have mercy on us.*
Christ, have mercy on us. *Christ, have mercy on us.*
Lord, have mercy on us. *Lord, have mercy on us.*
Christ, hear us. *Christ, graciously hear us.*
God, the Father of heaven, *Have mercy on us.*
God, the Son, Redeemer of the world, *Have mercy on us.*
God, the Holy Spirit, *Have mercy on us.*
Holy Trinity, one God, *Have mercy on us.*
Holy Mary, *Pray for us.*
Holy Mother of God, *Pray for us.*
Holy Virgin of virgins, *Pray for us.*
Mother of Christ, *Pray for us.*
Mother of divine grace, *Pray for us.*
Mother most pure, *Pray for us.*
Mother most chaste, *Pray for us.*
Mother inviolate, *Pray for us.*
Mother undefiled, *Pray for us.*
Mother most amiable, *Pray for us.*
Mother most admirable, *Pray for us.*
Mother of good counsel, *Pray for us.*
Mother of our Creator, *Pray for us.*
Mother of our Redeemer, *Pray for us.*
Virgin most prudent, *Pray for us.*
Virgin most renowned, *Pray for us.*
Virgin most powerful, *Pray for us.*
Virgin most merciful, *Pray for us.*
Virgin most faithful, *Pray for us.*
Mirror of justice, *Pray for us.*
Seat of wisdom, *Pray for us.*
Cause of our joy, *Pray for us.*
Spiritual vessel, *Pray for us.*
Vessel of honor, *Pray for us.*

Vessel of singular devotion,	*Pray for us.*
Mystical rose,	*Pray for us.*
Tower of David,	*Pray for us.*
Tower of ivory,	*Pray for us.*
House of gold,	*Pray for us.*
Ark of the covenant,	*Pray for us.*
Gate of heaven,	*Pray for us.*
Morning star,	*Pray for us.*
Health of the sick,	*Pray for us.*
Refuge of sinners,	*Pray for us.*
Comforter of the afflicted,	*Pray for us.*
Help of Christians,	*Pray for us.*
Queen of Angels,	*Pray for us.*
Queen of Patriarchs,	*Pray for us.*
Queen of Prophets	*Pray for us.*
Queen of Apostles,	*Pray for us.*
Queen of Martyrs,	*Pray for us.*
Queen of Confessors,	*Pray for us.*
Queen of Virgins,	*Pray for us.*
Queen of all Saints,	*Pray for us.*
Queen conceived without original sin,	*Pray for us.*
Queen assumed into heaven,	*Pray for us.*
Queen of the most holy Rosary,	*Pray for us.*
Queen of peace,	*Pray for us.*

V. Pray for us, O holy Mother of God.
R. That we may be made worthy of the promises of Christ.

Let us pray. Grant your servants continual health of mind and body, O Lord God. Let the intercession of the blessed ever-virgin Mary gain for us freedom from our present sorrow and bring us to the joy of everlasting happiness, through Christ our Lord. Amen.

About the Frescoes

Giotto di Bondone (1266 -1337)

Giotto was the first European artist to make a lasting mark as painter, sculptor and architect since the days of Greek antiquity. Before him, painting was still considered a craft, a "mechanical" art. In his lifetime, however, Giotto changed all that, and within ten years of his death was called by Boccaccio in his *Decameron* "the greatest painter in the world." In fact, he had raised painting to such a prestigious level among the arts that it influenced sculpture rather than vice versa. Giotto came to occupy a position of great respect not only in Florence, a city that was one of the most important centers of trade in Europe, but the impulse he gave to the arts was so great that it determined the destiny of European painting for several centuries. His rediscovery of the third dimension, of real and measurable space, of the natural appearances of surfaces, of the individualizing aspects of reality became part and parcel of European art for years to come. The frescoes that make up four of the five panels in this little booklet on the *Mysteries of Light* are from the Arena Chapel in Padua, Italy (Capella Scrovegni).

Fra Angelico (1400-1455)

Beatified in 1982 by Pope John Paul II, Fra Angelico was an Italian painter of the early Renaissance who combined the life of a devout friar with that of an accomplished artist. He was called Angelico (Italian for "angelic") and Beato (Italian for "blessed") because the paintings he did were of calm, religious subjects and because of his extraordinary piety. Guido di Pietro, his baptismal name, grew up in Tuscany and entered a Dominican convent in Fiesole when he was 18. He took the name Giovanni da Fiesole and began his career as an illuminator of missals and other religious books. He gradually graduated from that to doing altarpieces that soon drew the attention of his superiors. In 1436, he was sent to the newly renovated Dominican convent of San Marco in Florence to paint frescoes for the cloister, chapter house, and entrances to the 20 cells on the upper corridors. One of the most impressive of these is the Transfiguration, which is depicted in this booklet. In 1445 he was summoned to Rome by Pope Eugenius IV to paint frescoes for the now destroyed Chapel of the Sacrament in the Vatican, and from 1449 to 1452 he served as prior of the convent in Fiesole. He died in the Dominican convent in Rome on March 18, 1455.

ST PAULS

This book was produced by St. Pauls/Alba House, the Society of St. Paul, an international religious congregation of priests and brothers dedicated to serving the Church through the communications media.

For information regarding this and associated ministries of the Pauline Family of Congregations, write to the Vocation Director, Society of St. Paul, P.O. Box 189, 9531 Akron-Canfield Road, Canfield, Ohio 44406-0189. Phone (330) 702-0359; or E-mail: spvocationoffice@aol.com or check our internet site, www.albahouse.org